FINISHING LINE PRESS
www.finishinglinepress.com

The Snapping of the Stick

poems by

Aaron Lee Moore

Finishing Line Press
Georgetown, Kentucky

The Snapping of the Stick

To Donald Secreast,
for your unfaltering encouragement

ISBN 978-1-64662-237-5 First Edition

ACKNOWLEDGMENTS

"The Snapping of the Stick," *New River Valley Voices* 2018 Competition Winner
"The Graduate Brood," *Toad Suck Review* and *Poet's Haven*
"Venetian Vodka," Original Title: "Venice," *Virginia English Bulletin*
"Cult of Domesticity," "Thought for a Poem," *Miller's Pond Poetry Magazine*
"World of Warcraft;" "Cyber-muse," *Mobius: The Journal of Social Change*
"Anecdote of the Box," Arthur C. Ford's *The Pen*
"Trimming Texas Cacti," *Deep South Magazine*
"Depression," *The Stray Branch*
"So Little to Recollect;" "Maybe I Am a Lord of a Ring," *Poet's Haven*
"Bless You, Whomever You Think You Are," *Illumen*
"August, 2012, Tiananmen Square, Beijing," *Sandy River Review* and *Poet's Haven*
"Fail Well;" "White Trash Ennui;" "April 20, 2013, Lushan, Sichuan," *Toad Suck Review*

Publisher: Leah Maines
Editor: Christen Kincaid
Cover Art: Li Siying
Interior Photograph: Li Ya
Author Photo: Hu Qianlin
Cover Design: Elizabeth Maines McCleavy

Printed in the USA on acid-free paper.
Order online: www.finishinglinepress.com
also available on amazon.com

Author inquiries and mail orders:
Finishing Line Press
P. O. Box 1626
Georgetown, Kentucky 40324
U. S. A.

Table of Contents

United States: Appalachia, Virginia

The Snapping of the Stick

I killed a baby duckling
before knowing ducks could die.
Threw him up in the air
ecstatically above the blue
plastic pool till after awhile
he was gasping then slowed
then still. I ran down the gravel
driveway and kept running
till my sister caught up to me,
bringing me back, sobbing.
It came to me in a dream that night:
deformed, bat wings, un-feathered.
Buried not far from the rusted red
gate. After the grave was filled
with only a few handfuls of dirt,
the stark silence;

then, out of primeval compulsion
I snapped a stick and laid it gently on top.

The Holy Birth of Segregation

Childhood is an enchantment.
Deep down we all pine for regress,
that is, prior to our indoctrination
of Ideas;
when we learn how to segregate ourselves
from Others.

What about that golden era before "I" formation?
Those were the days…
when we're just marshy, spongy mush.
Not the faintest modicum of cognit
concerning the gandering apparition in that mirror,
floating about space without reason or rhyme.
Nothing to segregate the Self;
only the briefest beatific bit of *en-soi* unity.
We'll spend the rest of our harrowing lives
vainly in pursuit of a concrete nebula.
We are the dust of stars.
We are the illusion of philosophers.
We are the fabric of dreams.

Sitting on Santa's knee,
the velvet gave me goose bumps:
"Ho ho ho!" oh, the old perfunctory.
"What would you like for Christmas, my lad?"
The reply…
My mother's look of horror,
the Santa's face now hot red inflamed,
Wide-eyed, rose-rage chunky cheeks,
Santa had suddenly become far less jolly.
Dare I say irate?
But I just kept right on smiling,
Upon asking this Catholic Santa for a menorah,
Innocently enough.

The Graduate Brood

There's a peculiar nest in the sky
Having nothing in accord with Nature,
Where hawks and fowl pick their feathers out of compulsion,
Sustain themselves on their own vomit,
Strutting and fretting in fear of one another.

These strange birds read Chaucer, Milton, Shakespeare, and such
—But never Aristophanes—
Then hold a parliament of fowls
Where they squawk at one another
In crass cacophonous cackles.

Their seed cups aheap in millet, sunflower, dried papaya:
"Reason is virtue!" parrots an abstruse African Grey
Before knocking the head of another cuckoo
With the latest edition of Roy Flannagan's *The Riverside Milton.*

Sic Semper Tyrannis

If it's Weiss, take it twice
Or, perhaps even thrice.
He came from Mount Berkeley
In the late nineteen-seventy.
Such a bold analytic
And stuffy New Critic.

Public humiliation
Your decadent creation.
Papers painted red—
A constant source of dread.
Milton, Chaucer, Shakespeare,
You did so plain revere.
Tallied points of quizzes;
My love of English fizzles.
Syntax, diction, tone,
Explication-prone,
Formal elements thrive
In your New Critical hive.
The world of literary theory
Makes your discipline dreary,
Prescriptivism reigns
Lexicographer's chains—
An antiquated lectern bold
Thank God threw away your mold!

But something is now missing
When I'm on the fourth floor pissing.
Your office sadly hollow
Where are you to follow?
I had you beyond measure—
My own masochistic pleasure.

Five times I suffered through,
I can't believe that's true.
Yet I miss you like I miss an itchy boil—
The late-night incessant toil.

I finally found clear what at first looked dark
As an Israelite opening the ark.
I learned so much, and that was nice,
We will miss you, Dr. Weiss.

Venetian Vodka

In Venice I felt the sting
Of hunger, fatigue—
Overwhelmed I impeded
On European culture,
Marched into a café
To find a woman
Bolting back and forth
In disarray.

Isn't it funny?
Not to wear white jeans in winter,
To fall asleep on a train through the Alps
Having an old, Austrian woman
Stare in disbelief at you
For a solid three hours.

I was born egregious,
And I'm still waiting for the wolf
To pick me off and eat me.

But this tired young lamb
Collapsed in Venice,
Stretched thin by stinky water taxis
And crummy salty buildings.

I retired to my room—
Venice has deceived me;
But furthermore,
From the mini bar
I drank a mini vodka,
And it was only mini water.

Cult of Domesticity

American, Swiss, Cheddar,
Provolone, Parmesan, Brie...
Go ahead and scurry your little fingers,
Soft yet firm,
Through the grandly assorted
Castle of Cheese
At Publix

Your fingers scurry
Now, once as mine
Over moist, dewy nethers
—Sundry lands—
Sundry lands In The Beginning
Of an existence
Saturated by passion
Instead of assorted cheeses.

Our love has become
A Hickory Farms gift set,
But I doubt the honey mustard
Is enough to get me off.

Perhaps between the minivan
And the teddy bear-humping pug,
I could have found some pleasure
In the cold, concrete studio floor.
Perhaps the stains in the sheet
Could have sustained me
...a little more.

The cracks in the coffee cups
The roach food under the sink
The soap stains in the tub
The calcium in the pipes—
all so imperceptible
The dishes in the sink!

Is this the stuff that dreams are made of?
Is this my Breton Lay?
Achilles—you fleet-footed juggernaut—
You had it right all along:

Better to die young and full,
Far from your piss-ant town,

Than to die

A   Bored
                    Withered
                                        Domesticus

Thought for a poem

Thought for a poem,
And all that comes up are lines from Milton
And a life of abstraction.

Dichotomous, far very dichotomous…

Take that nail I pounded into the drywall,
Or that spark plug I extracted.

A life of movies and stories and old legends
—If Beowulf were alive now
He'd be waiting at the bus stop
Triumphantly yearning for the five tater tots he'll eat at lunch
And this time with ketchup.

Jolly Green Giants
Pasted onto cans of green beans,
And polar bears drinking Coca Cola.

Pray find your corner in these dying yawning breaths;
Pick the tags off of your mattresses
And unravel your gaudy turquoise sweater.

World of Warcraft

Inevitably
You always have those jerks
—You know the ones—
They slaughter you without mercy
Regardless of your low level
Because they can,
And instead of moving on
To some greater dark fulfillment
They park on your virtual corpse,
Just waiting for you to resurrect,
Your ghost suspended in the nether realm,
Hovering pathetically,
You waiting waiting waiting,
The ugly green orc parked patient with all the discipline
Of the Siberian Sniper.
He hefts his Tyrannical Gladiator's Decapitator,
Forged in the depths of Orgrimmar,
In fierce anticipation.
You are still waiting to rez,
Wondering the true extent of this tyrant's
Bored hawkish cruelty.
Still you wait,
The orc's unflinching face cool and keen.
Finally you rez…
He promptly kills you again
Doing what tyrants naturally do.
This is how the lonely Nationwide insurance
Salesman spends his Saturdays,
Sadistic and potent in his dreams
And so beautifully distracted.
If only we could gather all the

Hitlers
Stalins
Caligulas
Mussolinis
and motley such;

Place them in a dark basement with a lifetime supply of hot pockets
And set them to raiding and raping the innocents of Stormwind City
In the glorious desolation that is World of Warcraft.

White Trash Ennui

Grated Parmesan cheese
Falls lightly, sprinkles
On the chest hair of an unambitious one,
Who tried to punch a duck the other day
On the front of his dilapidated deck.

The coffee cups stained brown,
Beside the plastic black Blue Angels cups
In the virulent clot of dirty dishes,
With egg remains caked to the non-stick black pan
And flies that collide with fly tape
And sometimes a human being.

The boy that pisses out of his window
Kills the grass in a neat little circle,
Masturbates beside the white desk fan,
Gazes up at the stars at night,
Plucks at one with his finger
Till the mosquitoes turn him about.

The shotgun needs cleaning;
Shells spilled on an old lamp desk,
Splintered purple paint chips
Sprinkled

There's a Family Dollar now;
No need to kill the bear.

The Clothes Make the Man

An aquiline face,
Scattered carbuncles and warts,
The oily-dew countenance cries
You are evil, Summoner.

The white man smokes his Cubans,
His black obsidian top hat tipped to the side,
Lord Byron, my man,
A tiny top hat you are wearing,
And the bulge just above your ear
Is carnal and destructive.

The stevedore at the docks
Sees himself in the murky water
Fluid and dumb,
The sloping forehead speaks not of God,
His exalted forehead reached to the stars;
Your cranial angle has set you down
To a life of lifting crates.

Blankets our electoral appeal;
The candidates are ugly.
Far better if they were
Purely wrapped in bleached-white sheets
and speaking in Latin.

Was God ever writ in my face?
Surely His nose was not so pointy.
Sad I cannot make an offering
In the sandstorm in the ancient desert,
Suppose my divinity stoutly oxen
Or perhaps more precisely duck-based.

Somatomancy, Physiognomy, Phrenology
Words fallen from our lips
Yet sense retained,
Gripping my cotton candy stick,
Balancing my slender top hat at the elephant circus,
Adjusting my tie,
Shaving my face,
Wearing my Nikes,
Sporting my khakis,
Adjusting my package in the mirror.

Astigmatism

The plank of board
On the beloved ceiling
Of my barn
Bends towards me
This prompts me to believe
That beyond that plank of board
Is Void

Anecdote of the Box

I placed a box in Alabama,
And square it was, upon a mountain.
It made the lovely wilderness
Repel that mountain.

The wilderness fled from it,
And nestled away, extremely wild.
The box was square upon the ground
And short and on the land.

It took dominion nowhere.
The box was white and full.
It gave indeed of bird and bush,
Like everything else in Alabama.

Trimming Texas Cacti
In Memory of Grady Lee Moore

The words no longer carried any meaning:
"I am sorry for your loss."
So rehearsed and animatronic—
Like the pitch of a very bored salesman.
He had been on this earth 96 years
—Three dead lovers later—
The words such a stale, dead, flat and utterly useless gesture,
Like the majority of dead gestures in our cookie-cutter lives.

That very day less than 24 hours after his loss,
Like any good stalwart Texan, now retired in Tallahassee, Florida,
He who endured the wars and depression
Even the 1918 influenza virus that wiped out half his family
Mother included
In less than two weeks;
He who served as a refrigerator repairman in the navy during WWII
In the Mediterranean;
He who started the Grady Lee Moore trucking company
In Arlington, Virginia;
He who through good old-fashioned sweat and tears
Found success
And dreamed the American dream.

My gesture of sympathy dribbled dead out of my mouth
Only achieved meaning
In act
As we donned our gloves,
Marched out into the suburban jungle on Randolph Circle
And silently trimmed the overgrown cacti in his front yard
No tears
No remorse
Our motions long rehearsed,
Broken only by the occasional prick of an unanticipated spine.

Each spine a pang of undigested grief

Depression

Sometimes
It might
Just seem
As if
The world
Were sick-
lied over
In black
& white.

Maybe I Am a Lord of a Ring

Maybe my life is fantastic,
Typing away on this slender magic box—
The buttons I press—
The fountains spewing water—
The tiles of rock ripped from mother Earth—
These lighting fixtures glowing like individual Suns
Marvelous machines,
Components stolen from worlds away
And a faint perception of their majesty.

Maybe I am in a curious little story—
The crumpled up aluminum foil hotdog wrapper—
The multitude of shining planes paraded about—
The walls of the cubicle magnificent rifts
I can summon rainwater
With a tiny fire-starter,
Unleash a torrent and flood the halls.

Will I Be a Well-oiled Machine?

1.Will I be a well-oiled machine?
2.Just a little after far before not be?
3.Tediously calibrated?
4.So succinctly programmed?
5.Laboriously defined?
6.Completely
irresponsible?

Bless You, Whomever You Think You Are

I've spent an entire month now perusing
The cyber-archives of the Olympus Mons
Library here on Mars. Still ten questions
To every one answer regarding the strange
Rituals of the ancient Americans.

They died off long ago on Earth. The cause
Is still up for debate, a debate as
Tired as that between free will and fate.
Modern history teaches us some cultures
Seek their own self-destruction. It fascinates
Me—the secret, dark yearnings for the End
Of Days.

We've been hard-pressed in our research to find
An ancient culture whose quirky ritualistic
Behaviors exemplify more feelings of self-veneration
Than the ancient Americans.

A theocratic society in
Its inception, her laws and customs arose
Out of Judeo-Christian mythology.
Its early settlers even went so far as
To characterize the Americas
As a Promised Land spoken of in The
Bible, sought after by the Israelites.
In my research, what I find most indicative
Of these feelings of self-veneration is
Obvious: *In God We Trust* is printed clearly
On every bit of monetary currency unearthed.
Evidence to the contrary has yet to
Arise.

But all of that is old news among ancient
American historians in academic
Circles. I have found something worth publishing.
It took some digging through the archives, but
I found evidence of a simple gesture
Adopted circa AD77
Which remained in existence well up to
America's sudden collapse.

It seems that when an American would
Sneeze another would respond by saying
"God Bless You" or "Bless You" in a
Superstitious effort to ward off sickness.
The precise origin of this phrase is still
To this day unknown. This topic will make
For an excellent chapter in my dissertation:
Delusions of Self-Importance and
Personal Destiny in Early American Culture.

Fail Well

Be the best jizz-mopper you can be
Polish pristine the feculent bowl
Cook the clearest crystal
Pack a proper bowl
Consume the classiest boxed wine
Huff dust cleaner in K-mart
Date the chick with the furry upper lip
Sponsor an anorexic fun run
Drink champagne in your mother's Jacuzzi
Have bad sex
Be the sexiest virgin
Steal the most hotel soap
Trade food stamps for rice wine
Slay the most dragons
(In World of Warcraft)
Be the angriest Buddhist
Write the worst poem
Engineer an atomic bomb
Upgrade a cruise missile
Revise a better history
Oppose an assault weapons ban
Weaponize smallpox
Thrombose a hemorrhoid
Prolong your period
Circumcise your penis
Bind your feet
Cake your cavities in Betty Crocker frosting
Invent a condom for pandas
Discover a rabbit aphrodisiac
Oversee a glacier-melting campaign
Sell the most life insurance
Work for a health insurance company
Drive the fastest Geo
Grow a garden of weeds
Invent a new religion
Go fishing with a car battery
Feed pelicans TUMS
Calcify a cushion
Resurrect Stalin
Break up The Beatles
Protest the Peace Corps
Erase a race
Defenestrate a dictator
Pinch a most wholesome loaf

Needle Eye

The wavy metal sword,
Forged by the neophytic
Hands
Of a gap-toothed grease monkey meth-head,
Seems so distant now
Between the unfinished syllabi
And repeated bank statements.

Far away
The blundering knife fights,
Among children,
While the obese mother
Traverses in her green Chevy Neon
On a quest for 40 golden ounces
Of premium malt beverage.

On Sunday the fat bodies whirl
Like angels before God,
Pray through the grinding knees
For two consecutive paychecks.

Now, the cigar smoke haze mal-lingers
Like menthol smoke in a double-wide trailer,
Deeply haled and droll.

So Little to Recollect

Don't y'all remember Y2K?
It wasn't all that long ago,
But in the scheme of history our collective faces
Ought rightly still be red.

We pined for planes plummeting down to earth—
Murderous Mack trucks, sadistic soda machines,
Lawnmowers chasing down little kids
Like in Stephen King's *Maximum Overdrive,*
Or the less imaginative just for failed ATM's.
The poets among us for falcons gauging the eyes
Of belligerent falconers.

We all secretly hoped the millennial ball in Times Square
Would reset to 1900 and drop downward in flames:
Didn't we?

There were some holed up in bunkers
Outside Y2K compliant outhouses—
A lifetime supply of toilet paper,
The last feculent, mired scraps of civilization.
The meek poised to inherit the earth
And reorganize a new age-old paradigm
Using guns, saltine crackers, castles of potted meat.

We seem now to have little to recollect from that time,
Still little to learn from the year 999,
And the fanatical hysteria over one of the many Last Judgments
(It wasn't the first).
And so it all just keeps going round and round and round again and again
 and again
Because we have so little to recollect.

Requiem for My Dearly Departed Dentist

In a country where a dentist
can earn enough to buy an airplane,
I enabled my dentist.

Uninsured,
the money I'd saved up for half a year
as a graduate teaching assistant—
thousands of dollars,
bit by partial payment bit
trickled into his account,
paying so I could go on eating,
paying so he could go on flying,
funding his daredevil thrills—
the aerial deathtrap.
Drugs were never his kick.
He never prescribed me anything,
even after a bloody wisdom tooth extraction.

Then one day the plane,
like the crown on my mandibular molar,
malfunctioned,
brought him back down to earth
and smote him in the dust.

He died instantly in the crash—
a nice enough fellow,
he'd never shot any lions in Africa.
Conservative Baptist who told me
he would pray for me
when I left for Peace Corps.
I told him I could use all the help I can get.

I do sincerely miss him,
but I must concede:
blessed are the poor in spirit.

P.R. China: Sichuan, Chengdu

June 25, 2016; Xindu, Sichuan, P.R. China

At Guihu Park in Xindu
Where locals speak the serpentine Sichuan *hua*,
To my foreign ear sounding sibilant like s-s-snakes—
Heavy rasping s's, violently undulating tones,
Gentle buffer soft "h"'s all-too-oft omitted.
To my neophytic foreign ear sounding like heated arguments
In the hot summer sun, myriad and vociferous babel
Rising fierce across the languid rippling waters
Amid the sacrosanct rosy lotus petal tips
In the picturesque lake at Guihu Park.
Here the moment of an ancient poet, Yang Shen,
Who once pontificated this hissing *hua*
Better than most perhaps—
No Du Fu, Li Bai; nevertheless honored in stone.

What must English sound like
To the ascetic monks at Baoguang Temple?
We big-nosed, *da bizi*, foreign devil *yang guizemen*.
Tourists flutter about the sacred grounds,
Eyes cast downward on glowing iPhones,
Fortunes cast on plastic yellow cards,
In flowing red-lettered flowery Chinese script.
Hundreds of dusty, shadowy Buddhas peering inside,
Offerings of fruit imperceptibly rotting beside,
The *Gao Kao* Buddha a seasonal sensation;
Incessant prayers for excellent examination scores.
Tourists buzz about the vegetarian halls,
Scarce stardust flits of light in eternity—
"Petals on a wet, black bough."
The smell of burning incense
Pervading the corporeal
In the hallowed dimness of the evening.
The stillness of the air;

The stillness of the monk's chamber,
Silent—

Save the mosquito's buzz only faintly perceived
Trespassing the monk's tired ear;
Drowsily, he slaps a half-hearted smack
And outside short bowed brown old men
Practice water calligraphy on the stepping-stones,
The frills of the brush licking clean slate
Pontificating elaborate ideographs of meaning
Lifted away into the air within the hour,
Evaporated—
Wiped clean with all the sundry other
Works and days of hands.

2016年6月25日于中国四川新都

在新都的桂湖公园里
当地人说着绕口的四川话，
在我这个洋人听起来就像嘶-嘶-蛇—
“s”要狠狠地摩擦，声调得起起伏伏，
温柔的翘舌音，那软绵的“h”，往往被省略，
我一个老外，中文刚入门，听着四川话就像是激烈的吵架。
夏日的骄阳下，喧嚣声喋喋不休，
从泛着涟漪的慵懒湖面上热闹地升腾起来，
飘荡在桂湖公园如画的湖水里，
飘荡在神圣的莲花中，飘荡在粉嫩的花瓣尖。
杨慎，古代的一位诗人，
曾经对这嘶嘶作响的四川话发表过高谈阔论，
或许比大多数人都讲得好—
当然不及杜甫、李白；但他的文字也记载在石碑之上。

在宝光寺的苦行僧听起来，
我们这些大鼻子的洋鬼子
说出的英语又是怎样的呢？
游客在佛门净地来来往往，
盯着闪闪发亮的苹果手机，
命运写在黄色的塑料卡片上，
红色的谶语如行云流水，字体华丽。
成百上千的佛像蒙着灰尘，影影绰绰，凝视人的内心，
旁边供奉的瓜果默默衰朽、腐烂。
考试季一到，主司高考的菩萨面前，香客便络绎不绝，
企盼高分的祷告更是无休无止。
斋厅里，游客们吵吵嚷嚷，
鲜有掠过的微光，鲜有永恒的星尘—
“湿漉漉的黑树枝上花瓣数点。”
焚香之味
弥漫皮囊
尽在傍晚神圣的昏暗之中。
空气凝固，
僧人的居室亦凝固，
寂寥—
只有蚊虫的嗡嗡声可以隐约听到，

它们擅闯僧人疲倦的耳朵，
于是昏昏欲睡的僧人漫不经心地拍了一掌。
屋子外面，一些矮小的棕色老人弓着腰
在台阶上以水代墨练习书法，

毛笔的锋尖舔着干净的石板，
阐释精妙的象形文字之意义，
不到一个小时又全部消失于无形，
蒸发—
被其它杂乱的事物和劳作
清除干净。

August, 2012; Tiananmen Square, Beijing, P.R. China

"Long life, chairman Mao!"
Is the only English
My Sichuan girlfriend's mother can say.

I went to see him in August 2012,
That waxen preserved fecund
Sleeping soundly in his quartz crystal coffin.

Another sweltering day
In Tiananmen Square
Where dynasts once and future reign;
Where I witness the frozen corpse
Of an idea.

I read a book or two
On the communist's Long March
And naturally invested
In a novel underdog story.

I have seen the bullet holes in brick
At Kai-shek's temporary headquarters
In Xi'an,
Heard tell of the heroism of Marshal Zhang Xueliang
During the Xi'an Incident,
Former drug addict Manchurian warlord,
Who spent the rest of his life in exile
For doing one right thing.

Perhaps I'd stood in the world's longest line—
A sunny pilgrimage riddled with
Complacent smiling Chinese faces.
We sauntered our short lengthy march.

A sundry pack of poor peasants,
Bowed and scraped,
Chucked peach blossoms onto a pile
Within Mao's magnificent mausoleum,
To wither and senesce with all the other
Sweetly scented novel ideas,
Quietly yearning for immortality.

2012年8月于北京天安门有感

"Long life chairman Mao (毛主席万岁)！"
这是我四川女友的母亲
会说的唯一一句英语。

2012年八月我去看望了他，
一具精心保存的手饶蜡尸
躺在石英水晶的棺材里安然沉睡。
又是一个酷热的日子，
在天安门广场上
永垂不朽的君王统治四方；
我目睹这具冰冻之尸
凝结成了一个思想。

我读过一两本书
关于共产党的长征，
当然也花时间探索了
一则新奇的败寇轶闻。
在西安，
还走访过蒋介石的行宫。

目睹了砖墙上的弹孔，
听闻了西安事变中
张学良将军的英勇事迹。
这个嗑药成瘾的奉系军阀
只为成就一件正义之事
而流亡了余生。

或许我站在世界上最长的列队里
——一条欢乐的朝觐之龙，
到处都洋溢着中国人民满足的笑脸。
我们漫步于这短暂而冗长的征程。

三三两两的农民，
身躯佝偻、皮糙肉厚，
在毛泽东庄严的墓室前
将桃花抛掷，垒成小山，
随同其他馥郁芬芳的奇思妙想
默默企盼永生，
最后一起枯萎、衰朽、凋零。

April 20, 2013; Lushan, Sichuan, P.R. China

The
Day of the earth quake
Had Has a fine keen
Luster about it
*

The
Sheen Edges
Golden Of The
In A Clouds
Wreathed
*

Hundreds died that day
I cannot imagine their faultless faces
*

All Knew Knew.
I I
*

The x i e e t n w n ll
e c t m n k o i g I' DIE sOmEdAy BY SoMEthing-
*

Is it over?

*

The disrupt of routine—
Plans, calculations, earthen angst
Shattered, broken, fragmented For-Itself,
Rapture.
*

The preservation instinct
A solid postulation e
Put forth in fine, trembling certitud ,

Cyber-muse

Philip K. Dick was disappointed to find
That the government never wasted a second
Thought on him. All of his paranoia
Only fed his narcissism, while Richard Nixon
In all likelihood could not recognize his name.

I fly back and forth between China and America
Secure in my delusions of importance,
Imagining how the government officers
Must surely swoon over how unreservedly
Interesting I am. Surfing the Internet with me,
Boning up on our knowledge of crab apples,
Primitive trap door spiders of the Liphistidae family;
Posing questions like can you eat a skunk?
On a forum, with replies like why would you want to?
Is ambergris really formed from a sperm whale's digestion of giant squid beaks?
What's this inflamed goiter on my neck?
Am I anemic?
How much masturbation is too much?
What's the history of the word "defenestrate"?

Both countries now keep tabs on us all.
I only wish it were a team of anthropologists
Slowly digesting the puny pulp of humanity
With some scientific statistical conclusions to glean from
The myriad multitude:
Adorable cat videos, celebrity fodder, unanswered prayers,
Memes, motivational phrases, narcissistic blogs of feigned importance
And magnificent glorious porn porn porn—
I imagine it's mostly pornography, penis pills,
And cheap self-help ruminations,
Given what little I know of the human condition.
Surfing Wikipedia or surfing pornography—
Two different forms of masturbation?

Does *War and Peace* really hold up to interracial gangbangs?
Can we compare the *value*?
The French philosopher Jean-Paul Sartre once stated,
Whether one gets drunk alone or is a leader of nations,
At the end of the day amounts to pretty much the same thing.

This Race for Significance

Often have I pondered the moment,
recreated it in my mind likely
chocked full of anachronistic gear, equipment, and frozen faces;
the event where/when Norwegian explorer Roald Amundsen
(un)ceremoniously planted his flag in the frozen wasteland
as the first explorer to reach the geographic South Pole.

I can see climbing a mountain,
even if you see nothing but cloud at the summit—
some choice terrain more appropriate for
manufactured significance.
But the geographic South Pole?
A frozen, sterile desert virtually devoid of life,
where conjured-up lines of longitude begin/end
at an imaginary, undefined, irrelevant, geometric point?

Once when I was a stupid kid I ran back and forth
over the "border" separating Georgia and Florida.
But there was nothing there except a shot-up
emerald green sign.

Will future explorers set foot on the South Pole of the moon?
Will future explorers set foot on the South Pole of Mars?
Will we again stick yet another arbitrary flag
representing an arbitrary culture at another
arbitrary point on another arbitrary planet
patting ourselves on the back arbitrarily?

But you see it was all part of a *race*,
like Sputnik and the moon,
and therein lies the manufactured meaning:
the Norwegians had beaten the British,
and the British explorer, Robert Falcon Scott,
(un)ceremoniously froze to death in the snow,

disappointed, after his team
reached the South Pole five weeks
after Amundsen's team.
Nation against nation
in this race for significance.

Nothing seems to mean much of anything,
unless you compete in this simulacrated game
we like to play with ourselves,
and attempt to separate winners from losers.
What does it mean without that?
Maybe it's not supposed to mean anything.
Maybe it's all just *be*.
As the Chinese philosopher
Lao Zi postulated long ago,
以其不争,故天下莫能与之争:
Because they do not strive,
none may compete with them.

About the Translator

Xiao Shuang is a college English teacher in Chengdu, China. She holds a Master's in English Translation Theory and Practice from Sichuan University. She received a BA degree in English from Southwest Petroleum University (China) and graduated with honors. In 2015, she won the Third Prize of the English-Chinese Translation in BLCU International Translation and Interpreting Competition; in 2014, she was selected as a translator for Yeeyan Gutenberg Translation Project; in 2013, she passed CATTI (China Accreditation Test for Translators and Interpreters) English Translator Level II. She has worked as the coordinator and interpreter for Harvard China Student Immersion Programs—Summer 2014 and as an editor of *Sichuan University Alumni Magazine*.

肖爽

现为成都某大学英语教师，四川大学英语专业硕士，研究方向为英语翻译理论与实践；西南石油大学英语专业学士，方向为英语语言文学，评为"优秀毕业生"。2015年获得第四届北京语言大学国际口笔译大赛（一般性文本英译汉）三等奖；2014年入选译言"古登堡计划"图书翻译译者；2013年获得全国翻译专业资格（水平）考试英语二级笔译证书。曾任2014年四川大学-哈佛大学国际交流营项目协调员和《川大校友》杂志社编辑。

About the Photographers

Li Siying holds a Master's in Teaching English as a Foreign Language from Lancaster University, UK. As a customized traveling consultant after graduation, she has visited 37 countries, and established a travel-consulting studio in 2018.

李思颖

英国兰卡斯特大学硕士。现为旅游定制规划师，游历37个国家，2018成立旅游咨询工作室。

***

Li Ya is a college English teacher in Chengdu, China. She holds a Master's in Foreign Linguistics and Applied Linguistics and a BA degree in English from Southwest Petroleum University graduating with honors. Since 2011, she has worked as the business conference and negotiation interpreter for RPM Group (USA).

In 2013, she was selected as the volunteer team leader for 2013 Chengdu Fortune Global Forum. In 2012, she worked as the project manager for the Easy Pass China International Program in Southwest Petroleum University.

李娅

现为成都某大学英语教师，西南石油大学英语专业硕士，研究方向为外国语言学及应用语言学，评为"四川省优秀毕业生"；西南石油大学英语专业学士，方向为英语语言文学，评为"优秀毕业生"。2011年至今，担任美国RPM集团中国业务商务会议及谈判口译; 2013年担任成都财富全球论坛志愿者组长; 2012年曾任西南石油大学"走进中国"国际项目项目经理。

www.ingramcontent.com/pod-product-compliance
Lightning Source LLC
LaVergne TN
LVHW041558070426
835507LV00011B/1162
* 9 7 8 1 6 4 6 6 2 2 3 7 5 *